# Integrity

# Integrity

Leadership-Competence-Motivation-Success

**Progressive Youth Series**

Virender Kapoor

INTEGRITY
Virender Kapoor

Published by Qurate Books Pvt. Ltd.



Published in 2023



**ISBN:** 978-81-96261-87-0

**Qurate Books Pvt. Ltd.**
Goa 403523, India
www.quratebooks.com
Tel: 1800-210-6527, Email: info@quratebooks.com

# Table of Contents

# 1
## Personal Integrity

*If you tell the truth, you don't have
to remember anything.*

*—Mark Twain*

**BEING TRUTHFUL IS** perhaps the most important trait in a person, which not only makes him successful but also gives him a tremendous amount of self-esteem. A person of high integrity is always looked up to and respected by all the people he deals with. In simple words, it is the virtue of basing your actions on an internally consistent framework of principles—it is personal honesty. Once you have your principles in place, then you must follow them consistently in all situations.

Integrity is not an inborn trait, but of course, it is influenced by parental guidance, the environment in which one is brought up, and also the schooling one has had.

There is no such thing as minor lapse of Integrity.

*—Tom Peters*

## How Important is Integrity?

Would you trust a liar? Would you buy a product from a company which has a bad reputation in the market? Would you deal with a person or a subordinate who is not trustworthy? The answer to all these questions is a big "no." As one moves along in life and occupies positions of power, and a role of leadership—integrity becomes a very important ingredient for success. In fact, it is required from an errand boy to the CEO of a company. It is better to evaluate your integrity meter right from the very beginning and work to improve this trait. A person should never wait to rise up in the ladder in order to work on it—by then it may be too late.

## Cluster of Integrity

Integrity is a trait with several characteristics associated with it. Let us look at some of the most important ones first.

- Honest, trustworthy, ethical. A person who is high on integrity would be trustworthy and honest at all times. Such people are quite ethical too.
- Patriotic. People with high integrity are often patriotic. Conversely, people who serve the armed forces and live a disciplined life become patriotic and honorable. Remember, environment matters in influencing one's character.
- Upright stance. All those who have a value system in place stand out as upright people. They are not afraid to call a spade a spade. If required, such people do not hesitate to take a stand for what they feel is right.
- Genuine. Their approach is not artificial. In fact, those with high personal integrity are always loyal to the people they deal with. They are loyal to their bosses, their peers, as well as their subordinates. They are also very genuine in their outlook. Thereby, whatever they say, they mean it and abide by it.

There are many more qualities that are closely linked to personal integrity.

The following is the integrity cluster:

Integrity/Dependability

| | | |
|---|---|---|
| patriotic | dedicated | genuine |
| consistent | committed | deliverability |
| punctual | focused | industrious |
| honest | loyal | faithful |
| hardworking | sincere | devoted |
| trustworthy | reliable | righteous |
| responsible | ethical | upright |

> If you have integrity nothing else matters. If you don't have integrity nothing else matters.
>
> —Alan Simpson

In the armed forces, integrity is given very high weightage in officers' career progression. There are four star qualities which need to be rated in the confidential report or CR of every officer, and one of them is integrity. Any officer who fails to score full marks in this quality is never considered for promotion to the next rank. The air force unit of the United States similarly lays a lot of emphasis on high integrity for their officers. The simple reason for this is that high integrity means a high level of reliability that one can expect from an individual. It is not possible to have officers who are not reliable and dependable where the nation's security is at stake.

**Integrity and Pride**

Usually those who have high personal integrity are proud of the fact that they are honest and upright. They have high self-esteem and pride in general. The converse is also true in most cases—people who are proud usually have a high degree of integrity. The difference between pride and conceit must be understood closely though. People with integrity are proud but not conceited or snobbish. For instance, if you have a domestic help at home and you observe that she demonstrates high self-esteem, then you can also observe her behavior towards her personal integrity. Such people would also demonstrate that they are honest and dependable under all circumstances. The reason is very simple—they neither like to be ticked off nor do they like to be labelled as dishonest.

> Nobody can be so amusingly arrogant as a young man who has just discovered an old idea and thinks it is his own.
>
> —Sydney Harris

**How Does a Person Demonstrate High Integrity?**
Integrity is something that you either demonstrate or you don't. That is why, unless you score full marks on integrity in the armed forces CRs, you can't be considered as eligible for a promotion. It is like a woman is either pregnant or she is not; she can't be somewhat pregnant. People who possess a high degree of integrity demonstrate it in many different ways.

- They don't break promises. So, you can always expect them to keep their promises no matter what the situation is.
- They always are aware and proud of their honesty. That's one thing that they love to keep intact.
- They usually go the extra mile to fulfil the commitments that they make to others and to themselves.
- They take moral responsibility for their actions and do not believe in the blame game.
- Their actions are always congruent with their beliefs and what they say. This also means that they do not beat around the bush.

- Such people define their own internal value system, which acts like a guiding principle for them at all times. And they usually make these principles very transparent, which adds to their credibility.

Always remember, you know when you are doing the right things and you also know when you are doing something wrong. Listen to your heart and follow what it says—this way you will seldom go wrong.

> Real Integrity is doing the right thing, knowing that nobody's going to know whether you did it or not.
>
> —Oprah Winfrey

## Defining Your Own Values, Whatever They Are

Even those who don't follow the law of the land follow a certain code of conduct. Such people, within their own sphere, are men of honor. Even the mafia has a certain code of conduct. If they give their word, it will be honored.

In the film *Sarkar*, Ramesh Nagre (played by Amitabh Bachchan) is a person who runs almost a parallel government. He is the law himself and gets people beaten up, threatened, kidnapped, and even killed in some cases, if they fail to abide by the rules and regulations that he has set for them. He thus, successfully, runs an illegal business to earn a huge amount of money. He is once approached by another gang to get into drug peddling. However, he simply refuses to get into it. In addition, he also warns the gang that he would not even allow them to do drug business in his territory. These words were based on a simple principle that drugs destroy our next generation. He believed in this, and he refused the offer out rightly. Later, this refusal itself becomes a reason for his downfall, but he remains undeterred—he stuck to his principles till the end.

**Do it when Nobody is Watching You**

If you are following your principles consistently, then it shouldn't matter whether somebody is watching you or not. Your actions, behavior, and commitments must remain the same in all situations. You are not demonstrating or faking honesty to impress someone. You are actually honest to yourself and to the world at large.

Babe Zaharia was an amateur golfer who played in the 1932 Olympics. On one occasion, she penalized herself by two strokes when she accidentally played the wrong ball. "Nobody saw you playing the wrong ball, so nobody would have known, then why did you do it?" somebody remarked. She responded, "Because I would have known." This is one of the best examples of integrity.

Many times, we do things against our conscience, against our principles, even for petty gains. But in the end, it all squares up. You really don't gain a lot by doing the wrong things. If you had been upright and demonstrated integrity, you wouldn't have been much poorer anyway. Keep your word, choose the difficult right rather than choosing an easy wrong, and you will see the difference.

Integrity is what we do, what we say and what we say we do.

—Don Galer

# 2
## Organizational Integrity

**IN THE CURRENT** business scenario, companies doing businesses spend a huge amount from their operational budgets on advertising and branding. Most of the advertising campaigns project the products and services being sold as reliable and providing value for money. In addition to all this, every organization portrays itself as trustworthy, honest, and dependable. Millions and millions are thus being spent to build a fake image and organizational credibility. Companies thereby build perceptions in the minds of their customers, and these perceptions soon become reality in their minds. This entire process builds a company's reputation, standing, and credibility gradually. But this perception has to be backed by delivering the promised goods. Now if the organization fails to deliver what it has promised, the customers and clients would soon lose faith in them and stop buying their products. They will feel dejected and regret their choice.

How does this fit into the integrity scenario? Once the company has promised certain deliverables against a price and it fails to deliver them, the company doesn't have its integrity in place. In other words, it has failed to deliver what it had promised. In a competitive world, where a consumer has far too many options to choose from, a company that is low on integrity would possibly be the last choice on a customer's mind when it comes to putting their trust in it.

The supreme quality for leadership is unquestionably integrity. No succession is possible without it, no matter whether it is on a gang, a football field, in an army or in an office.

—Dwight Eisenhower

It takes years to build a reputation, but it takes minutes to ruin it. Can a company afford adverse publicity because it has failed to deliver what it promised? The answer to this question is a clear "no," because bad reputation spreads like a wildfire. Therefore, it is of utmost importance for an organization to build the virtue of integrity within its folds with dead seriousness.

The following must be done to ensure organizational integrity:

- Integrity flows from the top. Therefore, it is important to set the tone of ethical and honest behavior by the people in top management positions. All good companies do this with single-mindedness, and the results are evident.
- It is necessary to put in place effective, strong, and elaborate checks and controls at all levels to ensure integrity.
- If somebody wants to point out a fault in something or someone, then reprisal should be prevented at all costs. If this is not done, then nobody will come forward to correct the system. Which means, respect the whistleblower and don't shoot the messenger.
- It is good to provide training through seminars and lectures for the development of personal integrity and organizational ethics amongst employees.
- Ethics should be made an integral part of the work culture by introducing several reinforcements.
- It is important to create an environment of doing the right things. This can be done by encouraging right actions and also motivating or inspiring everyone to follow the right path.

- Good companies have a whistleblower policy in place to ensure integrity. If any employee feels that something is not right or something wrong is being practiced, he or she is free to blow the whistle and bring it to the notice of the authorities with immediate effect.

## The Story of an Honest King

Long, long time ago, there was a king of a province in China who was getting old, and therefore, wanted to choose his rightful successor. Instead of selecting one of his sons, he called all the young boys of the kingdom and announced, "I will give each one of you a seed. These are very special seeds and I would like you to take these back home. Plant these seeds, water and nurture them into beautiful trees for the next one year. After one year, come back to the palace and show me the results. The person with the best tree will become the next king of this province."

In the crowd, there was a boy named Hurang, who, like others, got a seed. He was delighted. He went home and planted it in a pot, used the most fertile soil available, and watered it regularly. He watched it every day to see if the plant had grown. He used many fertilizers in addition to ensure that the plants grew to be lush green. But nothing happened. After a month or so, the other boys started talking about their plants that were beginning to grow greener by the day. Huang, on the other hand, was left disappointed but kept on watering the pot diligently without losing hope. At last, he felt like a failure as not even a tiny plant had sprouted in his pot. After the stipulated time of one year was over, Huang refused to take the empty pot to the king, but his mother forced him to go. At the palace, there were a lot of boys, and all of them had exotic plants of great variety in their pots. Huang felt ashamed and stood in a corner while everyone laughed at him on seeing his empty pot. In the meantime, the king entered the hall and saw all the plants one by one. He then exclaimed, "Oh! Lovely plants." Finally, he reached where Huang was standing with his eyes pinned to the floor. The king looked at the boy and then he looked at his empty pot. He instructed him to come forward. Huang thought that the king would punish him; instead, the king gently asked him his name, and with a wide grin, he announced, "He is your new king and his name is Huang." Huang was shocked when he heard these words. The king clarified further, "One year back, I gave you all boiled seeds which would never grow. You all replaced it with different seeds, except Huang. He is not a cheat or dishonest. He is a man of high integrity, and therefore, is fit to be the king."

> I am very proud to be called a pig. It stands for pride, integrity and guts.
>
> —Ronald Reagan

## Famous People Who Had Personal Integrity

There would be hardly any successful leaders—political, social, or corporate—who lacked integrity. When you scan Indian history, you will get names like Narayan Murthy, JRD Tata, Dr. Kiran Bedi, Dr. APJ Abdul Kalam, Lal Bahadur Shastri, Mahatma Gandhi, and Narendra Modi who have demonstrated great personal integrity. On the international front, one could quote names like Dwight Eisenhower, Winston Churchill, Theodore Roosevelt, John F Kennedy, Jack Welch, and Lee Iacocca, to name a few, while talking about the effectiveness of integrity in one's conduct.

## Prime Minister Narendra Modi Gives a lot to Charity

Prime Minister Modi Lives a simple life. He does no favors to his family. His Mother who is 90 years plus doesn't stay with him in his sprawling Prime Minister's official residence but stayed with her son Pankaj Modi, a Gujarat government employee, used to live in a cramped quarter with Heeraba, earlier, which he later vacated. She has shifted to a new bungalow, which her younger son Pankaj Modi has built in Gandhinagar.

In 2019 PM Modi contributed Rs 21 lac from his savings to Safai workers of Kumbh Mela. He had paid 2.25 lacs to the corpus fund of PM CARES FUND.PM Modi's donations to public causes exceed Rs 103 crore. His prize money of Rs 1.3 Crore from Seoul peace prize was given to clean Ganga project and whatever gifts are given to him are auctioned and money given for charity.

## APJ Kalam's only property was his books and clothing

Former President of India APJ Abdul Kalam also known as 'The Missile Man of India' only owned 2,500 books, a wrist watch, six shirts, four trousers, three suits and a pair of shoes when he died in 2015. The Bharat Ratna awardee survived on the royalty received from the books he wrote and the government pension. Kalam, popularly called 'The People's President', was a simple man who had no greed for worldly possessions or money. He had dedicated his life as a scientist, researcher and a teacher. He never married and was wedded to his work alone.

Though a nominated president can avail free air tickets for his relatives attending swearing-in ceremony at the Rashtrapati Bhawan, Kalam, who led a modest life, chose not to avail such privileges and paid for 2nd AC train tickets for kin. Kalam invite as the "Presidential Guests" to Kerala's Raj Bhavan during his first visit to the state after becoming the president--a road side cobbler and owner of a very small hotel. Such people are grounded and are incorruptible.

## Abraham Lincoln

He was one of the most popular presidents of the United States of America. He was not only hardworking, patriotic, and well-meaning to others, but was a downright honest person. On one occasion, while he was managing a country store—when he counted the entire cash that he had at night, he found that he had taken a few cents more from one of the customers who was now gone. Without wasting another moment, and not caring about the night hours, as soon as he closed the store, he walked a long distance to reach the customer's place to return the excess change.

## Can We Make a Change in Ourselves?

It is highly important to understand that integrity cannot be taught, and one cannot give some quick-fix solutions for those who are dishonest, unreliable, and lack integrity. As I said in the beginning, although it is not an inborn trait, it can be learnt easily over a period of time through our parents, schools, as well as our friends. As adults, it is just a matter of realization of our actions that can help us include the quality of integrity in our conduct. It is an internalized process. If you feel you lack integrity and honesty, then first try to be honest to yourself. If you feel people don't trust you enough, then also accept this fact first to bring about a change.

Once you have accepted all the shortcomings in yourself, it's time to take a decision—a decision to boost your honesty, and in that process, develop your personal integrity. Ask yourself some hard questions, like: Do people trust me? Am I a dependable person? Do people believe in me? Do people respect me and my opinions? By answering these questions with utmost honesty to yourself, you will know if your integrity needle is pointing in the right direction or not and accordingly decide your next move.

Thereafter, you should make a list of a few cardinal principles for your everyday work and how you should deal with people you come across. Make these principles as simple as you can. For example, you may say these four things —"I will not cheat anybody, and I will do my best when a task is given to me;" "I will take moral responsibility for my failures;" "I will never make excuses;" and "I will be honest in my actions." Once you have the list, it will not be difficult to walk on the path of integrity. You have defined four simple principles, and thereafter, all you have to do is implement them in the best possible manner.

Once you have been able to practice these four principles for, say, a month, then you should add a couple of more such things from the cluster of integrity that we talked about earlier. This cluster will give your thoughts clarity and remove any confusion that you have in your mind regarding integrity.

> Live, so that when your children think of fairness and integrity, they think of you.

> —Jackson Brown,

The essence

Integrity is perhaps one of the few traits discussed in the context of emotional intelligence that is not a genetic bonanza or an inherited lottery in most cases. Although there are people whom we can call "born with a guiding philosophy of honesty." But to a large extent, it may not be applicable to all. In any case, if one is conscious of the fact that personal honesty and integrity are very important factors for a person's well-being, it is a trait that can be acquired with practice. To develop integrity, one requires more of mental or inner courage than physical courage that is required in a battlefield or a game of football or perhaps in the boxing ring. One has to prepare mentally, in order to become a person of integrity.

If you look at the integrity cluster, it clearly points to a person with strong and impeccable character. People who have led nations and corporations to greater heights of success, so far, were all men and women of integrity. A great engineer from an IIT or a business executive from Harvard Business School is worth nothing if he cannot be relied upon. Such is the importance of personal honesty in our lives. It is not only important to be honest and upright, but it is also equally important to demonstrate these traits in our day-to-day lives. It is also important to be honest when nobody is watching you, as these traits are not merely for show. Most of us would have noticed that Sachin Tendulkar—one of India's best cricketers—doesn't wait for the umpire to declare that he is out; he moves off the pitch the moment he knows he is out. This is the honesty that we all need in our actions. You would not like to play a hand of cards with someone who is a cheater.

Good honest people build good honest organizations—large organizations have perished due to the lack of organizational integrity. One should always remember that it takes years to build a reputation, but it takes only minutes to destroy it.

Building character and being honest and upright are choices we make as adults. It is as simple as that. Once you have decided to be honest and upright, thereafter things will automatically move in a positive direction and you will be able to practice and demonstrate honesty without any second thoughts. So go ahead and do it for your own good.

# 3
## Moral Courage

*It is curious—curious that physical courage should be so common in the world and moral courage so rare.*

*—Mark Twain*

HAVING THE COURAGE and guts to do what is right when faced with difficult decisions is the key to being a leader, a manager, as well as a good citizen. Unfortunately, today, many of us lack this courage. This is perhaps one of the most important traits of a good character and represents a dependable person whom one can rely on. This is also known as courage of conviction—which means to have the courage to follow your own conviction or your own value system, your own beliefs. This is also the biggest problem of our society—because people often fail to take a stand against the wrongs being done to them by various organizations, the system, and the powers that prevail.

### What is Courage?
Courage is being bold while facing any sort of danger. It is to stand ground in front of an impending disaster, loss, or calamity. Although

it is surprising to note, raw courage falls into two specific categories—physical courage and mental courage. Many people possess the physical courage to face a bullet, fight a boxing bout, look at death from close quarters, and are able to see bloodcurdling scenes and face the gory screams of helpless victims in case of a tragedy without getting too moved or disturbed about them. Such people have the ability to face pain, danger to life and limb, and uncertainty.

While physical courage is the ability to endure physical hardships, moral courage is more about acting correctly in the face of opposition, loss of job, facing a shame or a scandal. It is also probably the ability to sustain hardships and harassments over a long period of time. It is the culmination of moral values, realizing the consequences of following one's morals (this is highly important), and having, thereafter, the courage and guts to "endure" the consequences. It is the ability to stand up to your values and be prepared to "face the music."

In fact, the biggest problem in this process is facing the music. When we say, "Who will bell the cat," you may wonder, "Is it difficult to bell the cat or even a tiger?" No, it is not. But it is difficult to face the hurt if the cat decides to attack! Anybody can bell the cat if he is assured that the cat will not attack. In real life, nobody can assure you that the cat will not attack, so belling the cat becomes a problem in that case.

In simple terms, physical courage is the ability to hit out and moral courage is the ability to say sorry if you are wrong. Now, try to recollect an incident when you showed moral courage. Also write down the incidence in your own words—it could have been something during your school or college days or even during your later life, at your workplace or even home. Now do the same exercise for displaying physical courage as well.

> Moral courage is the most valuable and usually the most absent characteristic in men.
>
> —Gen George Patton

**Following Your Beliefs is Not Easy**

Having values and beliefs, and practicing them are two entirely different things. History is full of incidents and examples where the high and mighty failed to display the requisite moral courage. CEOs and CFOs of large corporations, who earn in millions, have kept quiet about financial bungling and misappropriation of funds in their organizations. Athletes have been caught for doping and drug abuse, even at the Olympics. Presidents, politicians, and rich industrialists have deceived the world about their sexual escapades. These are all examples of lack of moral courage during testing times or defining moments.

They lacked moral courage that lifts values and beliefs from theoretical discourses to practical center stage. In the good old days, politicians and bureaucrats would resign on moral grounds, taking moral responsibility for their actions or inactions. If there was a rail accident, and it was even remotely proved that it was due to neglect, the rail minister would resign. But will such a thing happen today? No. These days, people always look for a scapegoat or indulge in what is known as the "blame game"—it happens in America, in Europe, and in any and every country today. But yet, there are a few examples when people do rise up to the challenge or an incident where someone shows moral courage.

Moral courage for an ordinary man is to stand up against a dangerous criminal or a mighty politician by becoming an eye witness or giving their testimony, and thereafter, standing by their word in court. Fighting in a battlefield is raw courage and is an example of physical courage. Mahatma Gandhi, facing the British Raj and launching a long-drawn battle on moral grounds (prepared to go to jail and face insults, insecurity, and uncertainty) was the poster boy of moral courage. When Satyendra Dubey, an IIT-ian, became a whistleblower, or Shanmugam Manjunath from an IIM blew the lid, it was a display of moral courage. Unfortunately, both lost their lives due to their taking a stand.

Courage is the first of human qualities because it is the quality which guarantees all others.

—Winston Churchill

## Cluster of Moral Courage

| ethics | willpower | moral fiber |
| --- | --- | --- |
| values | confident | compassion |
| initiative | fearless | mental strength |
| leadership | altruism | family values |
| impartial | self-respect | trustworthy |

The Time Factor, Agony, and the Rewards

Yet another way to look at this is the time factor. Physical courage may be required for a shorter time, whereas mental courage is to sustain hardships over a longer period. For example, fighting two hooligans on the street may last for ten minutes, but the agony of fighting a court battle against a murderer may last for years—with threats, pressures, and bribes pouring in week after week.

Today, we also see great examples of demonstrated moral courage. When a poor women hands over her son to the police because he raped a girl is an example many of us are familiar with. At the same time, we have witnessed politicians, the rich and the mighty, and even senior police officers protecting their sons for the same crime. Journalists investigating powerful politicians or the mafia or the police are the highest form of moral courage. Many times, the rewards for the display of moral courage are not huge sums of money, but the contentment it leaves you with is unparalleled. Most often, it is mental peace, a boost to your self-esteem, and a voice deep inside saying, "Yes, I did it."

A journalist exposing a stock market scam gets only a scoop story—nothing else. A CEO going against the board of directors on moral grounds gets nothing—in fact, he loses his job. But yet people do it because they practice what they preach. In other words, moral courage is also walking your talk.

> Often the test of courage is not to die but to live.
>
> —Victoria Alfieri

## Valor of a Different Kind

There were instances of many heroic deeds in the battlefields during the World War II. There were also equally inspiring stories of courage—moral courage where people stood tall against pressure from all sides, knowing fully well that the consequences would be highly dangerous, which could also cost them their lives.

Dr Lazowski is a classic example, who saved more than eight thousand people from Nazi concentration camps—he spread the news of a fake epidemic, "Epidemic Typhus." He discovered that injecting a killed bacteria in a person's body would not harm the individual and yet the person would test positive for the disease. Subsequently, he infected many Jews like this and made the Germans feel that an epidemic was widespread. This way, a large number of healthy people were spared by the Germans from working under harsh conditions in concentration camps where death was almost certain.

He had taken a great personal risk here, because had he been caught for this act, his death was certain. He did this for a long time. At one point of time, the Germans suspected foul play and sent a team to investigate. He faced them courageously and warned them that they would also contract the disease if they stayed there for long. The team of Germans got so scared that they only took a few blood samples (which obviously tested positive) and went away in haste. Sustaining such pressure for a long time is required for moral courage of the highest order.

## Rewarding Moral Courage

Many companies have introduced policies to protect whistleblowers—the guys who report malpractice within a company. It is also time that we start giving out awards at the government level, as well as at local levels to reward those who display moral courage. Just like we have bravery awards for physical courage, awards for moral courage will help encourage people to come forward.

> Leadership requires the courage to make decisions that will benefit the next generation.
>
> —Alan Autry

## Valor in the Armed Forces

While army officers are trained at West Point in the US, Sandhurst in the UK, or even at the National Defence Academy, India—the focus is very much on physical courage. That is why a lot of stress is laid on outdoor games, boxing, cross-country runs, and physical endurance.

But are these training centers also building moral courage in their officer cadre? Many times, the top military brass looks at the young cadets as officers who would straightaway be deployed with troops in difficult areas, demanding physical stamina and courage to face a bullet after the completion of their training. There may not be a very serious assessment of moral courage. Even if there is, there is no focused approach to develop this trait in the armed forces.

Therefore, it may well happen (and it has happened in the past) that an officer valiantly leads his troops in a charge against the enemy machine gun fire, but fails to stand up to his seniors to object to their decisions, which could lead five hundred men to certain death. The 1962 debacle of the Indo-China War stands testimony to some such incidents. One would be able to pinpoint such follies in almost all the armed forces, across the world, and it is collectively known as "crisis in command." This is when even the senior officers failed to demonstrate a strong spine in front of politicians or bureaucrats, and many times, let their people die by treating them as dispensable cannon fodder.

A senior officer of the US army once said, "If you must sin, sin against God, not against bureaucracy. God may forgive you, but bureaucracy will never!" The same general who said this must have led his men in battle where it was a "quickie" as far as the pain was concerned. But facing bureaucracy is a long-drawn battle in any democracy and many generals fail to demonstrate enough spine in the face of it.

## A True Story of a Common Man

An engineer was employed as a quality assurance manager at Teledyne Relays, a company making electronic relays in California, US. This company manufactured relays and switches used in space shuttles, nuclear missiles, and very critical systems used by the armed forces. Malfunctioning of such systems can cause catastrophic damage—which can be unimaginable sometimes. Therefore, very stringent specifications are prescribed and very high standards of testing and quality assurance are required in such matters. Due to this, such components are very expensive—sometimes even ten times costlier than the commercial stuff. This engineer, during the course of time, realized that false reports were being given and proper testing was not being done. He reported the matter to his immediate senior. He was immediately asked to keep quiet and take no notice of what was happening. He felt that what the company was doing was grossly wrong, and he raised the level of his complaint by taking it to the vice president of production, but still to no avail. He was first transferred from the quality assurance and testing department, and later, he was sacked from the company!

This man never gave up, though; instead, he went to the FBI and reported the matter. Without a job in hand, he was facing a huge financial crisis and yet he was hell-bent on going to the FBI again and again. He had to go a number of times to convince the FBI that his company was indeed cheating the government and was into a big fraud. The FBI finally went into action, and the company was later levied a fine of $17.5 million, and then it settled losses by paying the government a total of $88 million.

> Courage doesn't always roar. Sometimes, courage is the quiet voice at the end of the day saying, "I will try again tomorrow" and not settle down as yet.
>
> —Mary Anne Radmacher

## Have You Ever Lodged an FIR?

How many of us have had the courage or enthusiasm to lodge a complaint at the police station? This complaint could be well for our own personal benefit or the society at large. Most of us don't even go for our own redresses because we feel that the police will not cooperate or will harass us even further.

How many of us have the courage to tell a person in the next seat to stand up in a cinema hall when he/she doesn't rise for the national anthem? How many of us have the heart to tell a person to switch off his cell phone when he is incessantly blabbing on the phone despite repeated requests from the air hostess before the flight is about to take off? Cross your heart and ask yourself for the right answers, and you will understand how important moral courage is in our everyday life and how much you lack in this aspect.

## The Enron Scandal: Arthur Andersen

The Enron scandal was a financial scandal involving Enron Corporation and its accounting firm, Arthur Andersen, which was brought to light in late 2001. Arthur Andersen LLP was once one of the "Big Five" accounting firms, providing auditing, tax, and consulting services to large corporations. The Andersen team handling the Enron audit directly contravened the accounting methodology approved by Andersen's own specialists working in its Professional Standards Group. In opposition to the views of its own experts, the Andersen auditors had advised Enron in the spring of 2001 that it could use a favorable accounting method for its "special purpose entities."

On October 19, 2001, Enron alerted the Andersen audit team that the US Securities and Exchange Commission (SEC) had begun an inquiry regarding the Enron "special purpose entities" and the involvement of Enron's chief financial officer, Andrew Fastow. The next morning, an emergency conference call among high-level Andersen management was convened to address the SEC inquiry. During the call, it was decided that documentation that could assist Enron in responding to the SEC was to be assembled by the Andersen auditors. Andersen personnel were called for urgent and mandatory meetings. Instead of being advised to preserve the documentation so as to assist Enron and the SEC, Andersen employees in the Enron engagement team were instructed by Andersen partners and others to immediately destroy all the documentation relating to Enron, and were further instructed to work overtime if necessary to accomplish the task of destruction assigned to them. During the next few weeks, an unparalleled initiative was undertaken to shred physical documentation and delete the computer files. Tons of papers relating to the Enron audit were promptly shredded as part of the orchestrated document destruction. A systematic effort was also undertaken and carried out to purge the computer hard drives and e-mail system of the files related to Enron.

In addition to shredding and deleting documents in Houston, Texas, instructions were given to Andersen personnel working on Enron audit matters in Portland, Oregon, Chicago, Illinois, and London, England—to make sure that all the Enron-related documents were destroyed there as well. No trace was left thereby.

On or around November 8, 2001, the SEC served Andersen with the anticipated subpoena relating to its work for Enron. In response, members of the Andersen team on the Enron audit were alerted finally that there could be "no more shredding" because the firm had been "officially served" for the documents.

Arthur Andersen was charged with obstruction of justice eventually. In 2002, the firm voluntarily surrendered its licenses to practice as certified public accountants in the United States after being found guilty of criminal charges relating to the firm's handling of the auditing of Enron, the energy corporation, resulting in the loss of approximately eighty-five thousand jobs. Although the verdict was subsequently overturned by the Supreme Court of the United States, it has not returned as a viable business.

## Collective Failures

Many times, it so happens that people show "collective moral cowardice." It could be a crowd of hundred people watching an accident victim lying on the road but no one coming forward to take him to the hospital or a bunch of people keeping quiet when a woman is being teased by a hooligan. I feel our society would be better off if people at least took charge collectively in situations that demands moral courage.

During the World War II, Germans were initially mesmerized by Adolf Hitler but were later terrorized by him to such an extent that nobody had the guts to oppose him. None of the Germans—civilians as well as men in uniform—opposed the atrocities of the Nazi party. Six million Jews were killed systematically under the garb of honor and for the sake of the fatherland, known as the "Final Solution." If Hitler was to be blamed for these crimes against helpless Jews, the Germans as a race were also equally responsible for displaying collective cowardice. None of them refused to drag screaming women and children to the gas chambers. How could they blame Adolf Hitler alone?

Later, after the war ended, during the Nuremberg trials, many officers pleaded against their crimes by saying that they were only obeying orders from their superiors! In a position of responsibility, you need to use your own discretion and not merely obey orders that are against your conscience. This requires moral courage. Many such failures have been witnessed during contemporary history, where people have shown collective failure of moral courage.

## The Moral Courage of a Child

At an age when children are oblivious of what morality is or what the word "ethics" comprises—Mahatma Gandhi, as a school child, displayed a great deal of moral courage in a strange way.

In his first year at high school Mr. Giles, an educational inspector, had come to inspect the school. The students were given five words to write as a spelling test. One such word was "kettle." Gandhiji did not know its spellings and had misspelt it. When his teacher saw this, he prompted Gandhiji to cheat from a friend's copy. He did not cheat as he felt it was wrong. Though he was later rebuked for not doing so, he remained undeterred. He was true to his values and showed moral courage even at a young age.

With age and experience, his faith in morality only kept increasing, and he followed his principles in every situation that he dealt with.

## How Relevant is Physical Courage Today?

There is a very little scope for physical courage in an organized society. One doesn't have to fight predators, nor does one have to get involved in street brawls. In fact, too much of bravado and demonstration of physical courage may land a person in unwanted trouble.

Battlefields and sports are probably the only places where physical valor is required these days.

Courage is resistance to fear.

—Marry Anne Radmacher

## The Importance of Moral Courage

This is one trait that is becoming more important by the day. Corporate leaders, doctors, politicians, designers, engineers, teachers, and soldiers—all need moral courage to do things in the right manner. Every profession requires ethical practices and behavior, and to practice values and ethics, one needs to have ample moral courage or the courage of one's convictions.

Once a group of students from an institute came to me to seek my support for a social cause that they were fighting for. They wanted to address a very serious issue through collective action, and later, wanted to give it the shape of an NGO which would take their voices and appeals to higher levels. They had a good cause to fight for and their efforts were united.

After listening to their impressive plans, I asked them to consider one question from my side—"How many students from your institute are prepared to give their lives for this cause?" I was not looking for a specific answer, but was trying to gauge the level of their commitment, the level of moral courage that they had towards their cause.

> The greatest test of courage is to bear defeat without losing heart.
>
> —RG Ingersoll

## The Story of Manjunath Shanmugam

IIM-Lucknow graduate, Manjunath Shanmugam, was shot dead on November 19, 2005, after he warned a petrol pump in Lakhimpur Kheri against selling adulterated petrol. The police found his body dumped in a vehicle in Sitapur.

His topic of research during his MBA and the topic that had caught his imagination was based on values. And he was ever willing to hold forth on the subject.

Manjunath—during his PGDM—wished for an HR exam every day; he loved to write about values and making a difference through his words and views. His favorite course in the MBA program was leadership. He spoke straight from the heart and hated any pretense in presenting himself—class discussions, interviews, anywhere . . . he just wanted to share his honest opinions.

Manjunath cherished simple values and honesty, and he fearlessly spoke about it. While the rest of his colleagues went in search of fat salaries and perks, he had opted for a job in the public sector as a sales officer in Indian Oil Corporation.

An IIM "product" visiting petrol bunks, collecting samples, teaching the staff some moral values like *"maalik nahi,* customer *paisa deta hai,"* were a part of his work profile.

He thought he could convince them not to cheat, not to adulterate diesel with kerosene. He thought making surprise visits would add probabilistic fears and deter such malpractices.

When he raised his voice against the prevalent activities, he was killed—murdered in cold blood. He was shot six times for having sealed a petrol bunk—a petrol bunk that mixed kerosene in diesel. He was brutally killed for having turned down the bribes that he was constantly offered, for shrugging off the veiled threats, and for having persisted with his . . . values.

By that yardstick, Manjunath was the truest of true leaders—because he really walked on hot coals to ensure the good of the masses. In the long run, we are all going to die, but Manjunath was just twenty-seven and murdered brutally for being a whistleblower. He died for something so abstract because society has lost its ethics and is now demeaning the "values" that it was once known for. People die for their country, their religion, and their faith or community. Then what is wrong in dying for your own values? Yes, it is as big a sacrifice as it would be to die for your nation. One should, therefore, not be afraid to stand by one's values.

## Can a Person Have Both Physical and Moral Courage?

Yes, they are not mutually exclusive, but they are also not mutually inclusive. It is not necessary that a man who is a great boxer or a kung fu fighter will be able to take moral responsibility based on his inner value system. It may also happen that a man who has tremendous moral courage to accept failure on his part will totally chicken out at the sight of a man with a knife in his hand.

Yet there are people who can show valor in the battlefield as well as stand up against a moral issue and be prepared to face the music during such defining moments where they are sure to face mental pain and agony over a long period of time. Such people are examples of being fully courageous—morally as well as physically.

## The Essence

Today we are witnessing an alarming deficiency of morals in our society. It is not that people do not know what is right and what is wrong. The problem is that everybody knows what ethics are, but very few people have the courage to practice these ethics and be prepared to face the consequences thereafter. We want to take the easier way out.

Raw valor and courage to fight in a battlefield or kill a lion in a jungle are not very applicable to all of us. In fact, these are the only places left to display physical courage today. But for progressing as an organized society, we need raw moral courage to perform raw valor,. In fact, these are the only places left to display physical courage today. But for progressing as an organized society, we need raw moral courage to perform well individually. Therefore, it is important to have courage of conviction. This is one of the most important traits of leadership in any domain—corporate, political, or otherwise.

It is not easy to follow your beliefs or put your values into practice. But we have enough examples of courageous people in all walks of life who have had the guts to stand up to pressure during those defining moments where others would have buckled under similar situations. We have had journalists, doctors, engineers, CEOs, CFOs, or even pilots and ordinary mortals, who, knowing fully well the consequences of their taking a stand, were ready to stick their necks out for the larger good.

There have been equally surprising examples of the high and the mighty who failed to rise up to an occasion when the world was looking at them and the people were looking up to them. They failed their people and they led their organizations to shame, and in many cases, to utter disaster. Surprisingly, many display physical valor, face machine gun fire, are prepared to pick up a street fight but become weak-kneed in a boardroom where they have to report financial inappropriateness or bungling, to say the least, in front of their superiors!

They fail to speak their minds—bureaucrats in front of politicians, executives in front of their CEOs, army officers in front of generals, and politicians in front of their public.

"Come to the edge," he said.

They said, "We are afraid."

"Come to the edge," he said.

They came. He pushed them . . . And they flew.

# 4
## Trust

<br>

*Trust is like a vase, once it's broken, though you can
fix it, the vase will never be same again.*

—*Walter Anderson*

<br>

**THIS IS ONE** word that moves the world—yes, you heard it right—moves the world. It is closely related to integrity and honesty.

Within a complex geopolitical environment, today nations don't trust other nations. Neighbors don't trust neighbors. For instance, almost the entire world doesn't trust China. India doesn't trust Pakistan at all.

Organizations perish if the environment doesn't trust it.

At a personal level, it can also move you comfortably within organizations if people trust you. It is important to build trust at three levels in the organization and at your workplace.

First is vertically above, wherein your boss and all the people you report to must trust you. It is also important that people senior to you in the organization trust you.

Second is vertically downwards—where your teammates who report to you trust you.

Third is horizontal trust—which means your peers trust you. For instance, a marketing manager must trust his branding manager or a finance general manager (GM) must trust the GM of the purchase department.

When people trust you, your work is done smoothly and you have a sense of self-esteem. You often say, "My boss never says no to my proposal."

## What is Trust?

- Being able to have a sense of security and confidence when dealing with someone.
- Having the ability to predict that someone will act in specific ways and be dependable.
- Earning a level of credibility that has built up over time.

But figuring out how to trust someone can also be as important as being trustworthy yourself. It is not easy.

I feel trust is more from the heart than the head. When a soldier goes into the battlefield, he has to trust his officer, not only about his competence but also that he would not be abandoned by his comrades and commanders in difficult situations.

Unfortunately, the statistics show that people trust each other less today than forty years ago.

At an individual level, you need to have mutual trust with your romantic partners, family members, and friends.

> Consistency is the true foundation of trust. Either keep your promises or do not make them.
>
> —Roy T Bennett

## Building Blocks of Building Trust

1. Honesty is the best policy. To be honest in your dealings is the most important part of building trust. How can someone trust you if you are not honest—that is the basic premise.
2. Keep your promises. This is very important to gain the trust of friends, colleagues, family, and even business associates.
3. Be consistent. You goof up once, and your entire reputation goes out of the window. So be careful as to never do anything that would jeopardize your trust.
4. If you are wrong, admit it. This builds your reputation and earns you trust and respect amongst all those whom you deal with.
5. Two-way communication is important. Communicate your point clearly and leave no doubts in the other person's mind as to what you want to convey. Many times, not choosing the right words can create misunderstanding.
6. Be genuinely good to others. If you help people without an agenda, you win over hearts forever.
7. Relate to people at a personal level. If you remember what the favorite color or favorite drink of a person is, he will be delighted. Try to remember the names of children of your colleagues—this helps. Some people have a great memory for names; those who don't, must make efforts. I do not have a good memory for names and it can be embarrassing.
8. Stick to your values. This is important. Even if you are alone in your opinion, don't back off. Also, stand up for the right thing and do not be a part of the crowd.
9. Don't hide things. Be as transparent as possible. How do you expect others to trust you if you don't trust others?
10. Say why you are doing what you are doing. People must know your intentions and your thought process.
11. Under-promise and overdeliver.

12. Stick to time lines.
13. Never lie.

> Whoever is careless with the truth in small matters cannot
> be trusted with important matters.
>
> —Albert Einstein

Trust is a long-term investment in relationships and it takes a long time to build it.

Another important aspect is that if you fool around, people stop trusting you.

## The Story of a Sheperd Boy

We all have heard this story in school when we were young. It is important to repeat it here.

A shepherd boy looked after his master's sheep near a thick forest not far from his village. Soon he found life in the pasture very boring and monotonous. All he could do to amuse himself was to talk to his dog or play on his shepherd's pipe or just whistle along aimlessly.

One day, as he sat watching the sheep and the quiet forest, and thinking what he would do should he see a wolf, he thought of a plan to amuse himself.

His master had told him to call for help should a wolf attack the flock, and the villagers would drive it away. So now, though he had not seen anything that even looked like a Wolf, he ran towards the village, shouting at the top of his voice, "Wolf! Wolf!"

As he expected, the villagers who heard the cry left their work and ran in great excitement to the pasture. But when they got there, they found the boy doubled up with laughter at the trick he had played on them.

A few days later, the boy again shouted, "Wolf! Wolf!" Again the villagers ran to help him, only to be laughed at again.

Then one evening, as the sun was setting behind the forest and the shadows were creeping out over the pasture, a wolf *really* did spring from the underbrush and attack the sheep.

In fear, he ran towards the village shouting "Wolf! Wolf! Please help." Though the villagers heard the cry, they did not run to help him as they had before. "He cannot fool us again," they said.

The wolf killed a great many of the sheep and then slipped away into the forest. His master fired him from the job and he became jobless.

The moral of this story is:

Once trust is broken you lose your credibility.

It is important not to fool around with people as it can land you in real trouble in times of a crisis. You also lose face and people don't take you seriously once they come to know your wrong intentions—they stop trusting you.

> We're paying the highest tribute you can pay a man. We trust him to do right. It's that simple.
>
> —Harper Lee, *To Kill A Mockingbird*

Conversely, strong trust can become a faith when it is at an emotional level. Here is a true story of two friends, James and Adam, who were childhood friends and went to the same school. They had known each other's families and joined the army. As luck would have it, James and Adam joined the same regiment. The war stared and their regiment was deployed in the thick of the battle. There was heavy shelling from the enemy side and many soldiers got killed on both sides.

As they were advancing, James got injured and stuck in an open trench, and Adam, with the rest of the platoon, could reach a safe bunker some distance away. The shelling became more intense, and

Adam thought that unless James was evacuated, he would not survive. He wanted to run up to the open trench in the middle of the heavy shelling, but his colleagues told him not to go as it was not safe to step out of the bunker. Adam couldn't abandon his friend, and therefore, ran to the trench through the heavy shelling. He managed to reach the trench unscathed and jumped inside to tend to James, who was badly wounded but still alive. He was breathing heavily and was so badly injured that Adam thought he would not survive and took him in his arms. Before James died, he said, "Adam, I knew you would come to rescue me!" At this, Adam cried profusely.

All along, James had trusted Adam to come to his rescue—this was the strong emotional bond and mutual emotional trust between the friends.

> You can fool some of the people all of the time, and all of the people some of the time, but you cannot fool all of the people all of the time.
>
> —Abraham Lincoln

# 5
## Reliance and Certitude

**Indians Who Are the Most Trusted by Indians**

*I don't believe in taking the right decisions.*
*I take decisions and then make them right.*

*—Ratan Tata*

***READERS DIGEST* MAGAZINE** had conducted a survey to determine the top ten Indians who were trusted the most. Let me pick up a few from the top ten, and let us gloss over some salient features of these personalities from different professional backgrounds. They inspired Indians the maximum.

People loved and respected the former president of India, Late APJ Abdul Kalam and voted him at number one. Ratan Tata, Narayan Murthy, and Kiran Bedi too were in this list.

Let us have a look at their work and the contributions that they made to earn the respect and trust of people.

If you want to shine like a sun, first burn like a sun.

—APJ Abdul Kalam

## Dr. APJ Abdul Kalam

Born to a poor family in Tami Nadu, he had a difficult childhood in terms of comforts. He used to sell newspapers to help the family survive. He learnt discipline from his father and kindness from his mother. He wanted to become a pilot but failed to qualify and wanted to do something related to aircraft and flying. He did aerospace engineering from Madras Institute of Technology, and he worked with HAL as a trainee and learnt the work hands-on. He joined the Defence Research Development Organisation (DRDO). Later, he joined Indian Space Research Organisation (ISRO) as a rocket engineer, and that was the path that led him to associate completely with the Indian space program and earned him the title of "Rocket Man." He was a simple person and always encouraged his team members to take risks, and they could trust him for his support and guidance. He was a consistent performer and was later made the principle scientific advisor to the Government of India. The Indian space program and the rockets we can boast about were all due to his vision and hard work. He was elected the eleventh president of India by the NDA government and was unanimously voted by the opposition too.

He donated his entire salary for public good to an NGO. After retirement, he began meeting youth and teaching, which he loved.

He was fond of reading and writing. He wrote many books for youth and about his vision of India. He never amassed any wealth and had very few belongings, including a wristwatch and two trunks full of books and only half a dozen trousers and shirts for his personal use. A great man, he was later awarded the Bharat Ratan—the highest civilian award. He was a simple man whom the country respected, and above all, trusted to the hilt.

**Ratan Tata**

> Business, as I have seen it, places one great demand on you:
> it needs you to self-impose a framework of ethics, values,
> fairness and objectivity on yourself at all times.

> —Ratan N Tata, 2006

The Tata Group has always stood for honesty, trust, and integrity. Ratan Tata too took that flag forward and demonstrated to the world that one can succeed in business with honesty and fair play.

Tata has always been a value-driven organization. These values continue to direct the growth and business of Tata companies.

Five core values of the group are:

Integrity
We will be fair, honest, transparent and ethical in our conduct; everything we do must stand the test of public scrutiny.

Responsibility
We will integrate environmental and social principles in our businesses, ensuring that what comes from the people goes back to the people many times over.

Excellence
We will be passionate about achieving the highest standards of quality, always promoting meritocracy.

Pioneering
We will be bold and agile, courageously taking on challenges, using deep customer insight to develop innovative solutions.

Unity
We will invest in our people and partners, enable continuous learning, and build caring and collaborative relationships based on trust and mutual respect.

A Padma Bhushan and Padma Vibhushan awardee, philanthropist, and one of the most successful businessmen the country has ever produced, Ratan Tata's legacy speaks for itself.

He graduated from the Riverdale Country School in New York City and received a degree in architecture with structural engineering from Cornell University, US. He later enrolled at the Harvard Business School and completed an advanced management program in 1975.

Under his leadership, Tata Sons' revenue grew over forty times and profit over fifty times. He was instrumental in the business of popular cars like the Tata Nano and the Tata Indica. He got Tata Tea to acquire Tetley, Tata Motors to acquire Jaguar Land Rover, and Tata Steel to acquire Corus, and in 2004, Tata Motors was even listed on the New York Stock Exchange.

Ratan Tata donated $50 million to his alma mater, Harvard Business School, for the construction of an executive center. He also gave Rs.950 million to IIT, Bombay, the largest donation received in its history, and formed the Tata Centre for Technology and Design to develop design and engineering principles suited to the needs of people and communities with limited resources. The Tata Group formed the MIT Tata Center of Technology and Design at the Massachusetts Institute of Technology to address the hurdles faced by communities with limited resources. It also donated Rs.1,500 crore to help India fight the coronavirus pandemic this year.

A great philanthropist, he has given most of his wealth towards charity, education, and the health sector.

I remember some years ago while boarding a flight from Pune airport, I saw a tall man wearing a suit, pushing his own luggage on a trolley, and waiting in the queue for his turn to get into the airport. His face looked familiar, and as I came closer, I was left speechless. The man pushing the luggage cart was none other than Mr. Ratan Tata! Imagine a billionaire and such a famous person had no flunkies around him and no one to assist him, and he is an elderly person, at least seventy-plus in those days. This is known as class and real simplicity, which surely percolates down the organization.

The Tata brand's distinction is the trust of society earned by the values by which the Tata group and its companies operate.

An incident mentioned by a very senior employee, Arun Maira, of the Tata Group is worth narrating in brief. He says (input given to *Mint*) that in 1970, Tata set up their first production facility in Malaysia. The business didn't do well and the bank gave them a notice to wind up as the loans could not be paid. A senior banker came to their Mumbai office to deliver the ultimatum. All Tata Motors could do was to give a one-page letter of assurance signed by the CEO that they would do their best to repay the loan and would make all efforts to boost the business.

The banker wondered what that piece of paper and its assurance was worth. So he asked Deutsche Bank in Germany, who had been bankers to the Telco joint venture with Daimler Benz. The bank told him that a letter signed on the Tata letterhead by the CEO of a Tata company was better than the financial guarantee of a bank! And everything got sorted out. This is the power of trust.

I once had a problem with a very senior person in Tata Communication and a meeting for which I had traveled to Delhi was cancelled without me being informed. The worst was that no one bothered to redress my agony. I was upset and decided to write a letter to Mr. Ratan Tata narrating the incidence. Within a few days, I got a response from his office regretting the incident and promising to take corrective action! This earned the entire group tremendous respect in my eyes.

## Mr. Narayan Murthy

> You do not have to be the son of a rich man to be an entrepreneur. Today kids are far more willing to take risks because they've seen high rewards.
>
> —NR Narayana Murthy

Organizations are not brick and mortar—that comes later. First are the people who bring ideas intellect, value, and vision.

That is what was done by a gang of young IT professionals, which included Narayan Murthy. All these youngsters were from a middle-class background but very hardworking, passionate, and well educated. Murthy had worked as a research assistant at IIM, Ahmedabad and later worked as a systems programmer. With sufficient hands-on IT experience and a small, failed venture under his belt, he joined Patni Computers at Pune, from where his journey began. He along with some others from the same company started Infosys in 1981, when computers were pretty new to India. They had no money so Narayan Murthy borrowed Rs.10,000 from his wife to start the venture. They wanted to build a company not only for profits but for creating wealth for investors and employees too. That was their focus and was reflected in their vision, mission, and working tag line as given below.

Infosys' Mission Statement

To achieve our objectives in an environment of fairness, honesty, and courtesy towards our clients, employees, vendors and society.

Infosys' Vision Statement

To be a globally respected corporation that provides best-of-breed business solutions, leveraging technology, delivered by best-in-class people.

Infosys Tagline
Powered by Intellect, Driven by Values.

After an initial struggle and a newly formed marketplace, the company started picking steam.

Infosys touched US $100 million in 1999. It also became the first IT company from India to be listed on NASDAQ.

The share price of the firm surged to Rs.8,100 by 1999, making it the costliest share of the time. At that time, Infosys was among the twenty biggest companies by market capitalization on NASDAQ.

Murthy served as the CEO of Infosys for twenty-one years—from 1981 to 2002—and was succeeded by cofounder Nandan Nilekani. At Infosys, he articulated, designed, and implemented the Global Delivery Model for IT services outsourcing from India. He was the chairman of the board from 2002 to 2006, after which he also became the chief mentor. In August 2011, he retired from the company, taking the title chairman emeritus.

By 2017, Infosys had hundred and sixteen development centers across the globe along with eighty-four sales and marketing offices. Its major presence is in India, United States, China, Australia, Japan, and Europe.

Murthy wanted to make thousands of his employees, drivers, plumbers, electricians, and IT professionals into millionaires, which he did. By the end of 2000, Infosys had hundred billionaires (In Rupees) and two thousand plus millionaires in their fold.[1]

The markets trust them, the government trusts them, and even employees trust them and are loyal to him.

## Dr. Kiran Bedi

She was the first woman Indian Police Service (IPS) officer in the year 1972.

---

1 https://timesofindia.indiatimes.com/at-infosys-drivers-electricians-are-millionaires/articleshow/16846079.cms

Just to put the record straight, there are twenty-eight director generals of police (DGP), one in each state in India, and eight DGsP (Director Generals of Police) in the Union Territories (UT) in India, and several other DGP rank officers in other assignments. The number goes well beyond forty.

Kiran Bedi rose to the rank of DGP, and is probably the only police officer remembered and respected by the people, especially the youth of India. An avid tennis player, totally upright as an officer, and known for her no-nonsense attitude, she would treat everyone as equal in front of the law and was ready to take up the cudgels with even powerful politicians and bureaucrats. She brought several reforms in Tihar Jail in Delhi as inspector general (IG), prisons. She had also championed the cause of fighting drug abuse and created several detox centers.

She was overlooked for the post of DGP Delhi and resigned in 2007, citing personal reasons. She joined Anna Hazare's India Against Corruption (IAC) movement and later joined BJP and served as lieutenant governor (LG) of Puducherry. She gave TEA as the mantra for transformation—Trust, Empowerment, Accountability—to the staff and the government. She used to conduct surprise checks as LG , many times traveling on a two-wheeler or even in public transport.

So many serve the IPS, but very few gain the respect and trust of people like she did. She gained the trust of people over a long forty years of public service

> I had a clear vision: if I take up an assignment, I'll do full justice to it; otherwise I'll walk away.

> —Kiran Bedi

# 6
## Dependability

*Gain a modest reputation for being unreliable and you
will never be asked to do a thing.*

*—Paul Theroux*

**WITH MORE THAN** thirty years of experience in grooming, mentoring, and making MBA students job ready and also handling the placement process at Symbiosis as a director, I learnt one major lesson—that today the industry is struggling to get a dependable workforce. I have been constantly dealing with HR heads and CEOs of companies small and big, assessing the performance of managers and eagerly taking feedback on the performance of our students on a regular basis. The major pain point is that most employees want great salaries but are not prepared to work sincerely and most are not even responsible in their behavior and performance.

This sends one clear message to the entire young generation that is looking for employment. If you want a job and want to stick to it, getting your regular increments and great appraisals, you need to become a dependable worker in the workforce—period.

It is very simple. Can people rely on you and can people count on you is what counts at the end of the day. If you have a colleague or a teammate, won't it be wonderful that once you have given him/her a task you can be rest assured it will be done to your satisfaction and on time. Yes, if your entire team is like that, whom you can count on, you will be the happiest person. Even in military operations, you take your best people with you for critical missions. You want a fail-safe team, a team you can count on. Even a weapon has to be fail-safe! It should not let you down at the last moment in the battle. It could cost you your life. The Israeli-made Uzi submachine gun has been one of the most dependable and reliable weapons and has been adopted by more than ninety countries. Amongst pistols, the most reliable are the Glock 19 and CZ P10C, and professionals swear by these.

At work, being a dependable person is the most sought-after quality in an organization. You have to be consistently dependable. If you're wondering how to be dependable at work, it's essential to focus on what needs to get done and make sure no part of a project gets out of hand. If you can work consistently with this mindset, you'll be a dependable employee who can accomplish almost anything.

Always keep the idea of interim feedbacks as an important tool in your dependability toolbox.

If you have been given a task which has to be submitted the next day at 10:00 a.m., and let's say you are getting delayed for reasons best known to you, then it is good to inform your boss/supervisor about the delay in the evening, seeking more time to complete it, rather than telling him next day at 10:00 a.m. that the job could not be finished. As a good practice, even if the work is going as per schedule, it is better brief your boss before the end of the day, so that he gets feedback without asking. Remember, you are there to assist the team and team leader in accomplishing the task and making things work well and on time.

One way to do this is by planning your day and time better. Good planning helps you to be organized and helps you avoid wasting time.

Some people prefer to write schedules down, while others prefer to use their phones or tablets. Make the most of your time and don't let little things slip through the cracks

Please remember that these things matter a lot, and in a competitive work environment, this helps you in more ways than one.

Don't make any promises that you cannot keep.

—Ann Marie Aguilar

If you are a manager, you need to be dependable too. Your team looks up to you and also depends on you.

Communication is the bedrock of dependability. Whether you command a small team or are at the helm of an organization, be sure to clearly convey your needs and expectations. Don't assume people know what you want them to do if you don't tell them. Don't ever confuse people, and always be accessible.

Listening to everyone is also important. There is a need to listen to everyone, even critics or employees who have a different way of doing things. Successful managers find solutions to problems by thinking outside the box and not just relying on what's worked before. They hold themselves accountable to their teams. They make sure that employees feel they have a say in the smooth running of the office. The dependable manager is always willing to lend an ear to a colleague. Sometimes you get brilliant ideas and points you could have missed.

Be a guide and a mentor to be counted as a dependable manager. Your employees may not see the big picture at all times, but you can see it from your vantage point. When the chips are down, it's more important than ever to direct the team's sights on the forest, not the trees. A positive approach to problems creates stability, which can be an essential component of dependability.

Along with guiding, planning and goal setting go a long way towards success. If your team knows what it's working towards, with clear timelines and goals, they'll have a path to follow. Clarity of direction sets you up as a dependable leader.

If you are an entrepreneur or running even a small tailoring business or a carpenter's workshop, you will do well—in fact, very well—if you deliver on time.

In India, most of us do not respect time and timely completion of projects. Now, it has become an acceptable norm—a *"sab chalta hai"* attitude. But never when you are working in a global environment, where this is unacceptable. If you do not complete a project on time, rest assured you will not get any more projects.

It is sad that our road building and bridge building always take more time than planned/promised. Builders don't complete projects on time and buyers are left in the lurch. Therefore, make this a habit. If a tailor doesn't stitch your shirt on time, you will never go to him again, right?

For large-sized projects, it is good to plan all the details and line up the resources, approvals, material, and manpower to be in position at the time of commencement of the work. It is better to keep an adequate cushion in the estimate.

With this as your business mantra make it like your unique selling proposition (USP) and your signature style—always on time and always the best.

> Ability is a wonderful thing, but its value is greatly enhanced by dependability. Ability implies repeatability and accountability.
>
> —Robert A Heinlein

# 7

## Questions to Answer

1. Why is integrity important? Justify with an example from real life.
2. Give ten traits from the integrity cluster.
3. How does a person demonstrate that he is a man/woman of integrity?
4. Name two great organizations that, according to you, have great integrity. Justify your answer.
5. Name three people who you feel are men/women of integrity. Justify each case.
6. Can you cultivate integrity? Give a brief plan for yourself.
7. What is moral courage? How is it different from physical courage?
8. Write down ten traits from the cluster of moral courage.
9. Recount a story of moral courage from your experience.
10. What is the basis of trust? Why did people distrust others more than forty years ago?
11. Enumerate seven building blocks of building trust.
12. Narrate the story of a friend who you feel you can trust and why.
13. Name five people from public life you trust.
14. What do you understand by being a dependable person and how can you make this your USP in your workplace?
15. How does an organization do better than others in a competitive market by demonstrating dependability?

# A Note for Readers

As they say, if you have integrity, nothing else matters, and if you do not have integrity, nothing else matters! Surely, there is a lot of substance in this statement, and let me substantiate this by saying that integrity has at least three more values within its fold. I have included all these traits in this short book.

These are moral courage, which complements integrity and trust, and dependability flow out of these two ie moral courage and integrity.

Therefore this book gives you a 360-degree perspective of integrity.

Happy reading
Virender Kapoor